How Do We Think?

Carol Ballard

RSVP
**RAINTREE
STECK-VAUGHN**
P U B L I S H E R S
The Steck-Vaughn Company

Austin, Texas

How Your Body Works

How Do Our Eyes See?

How Do Our Ears Hear?

How Do We Taste and Smell?

How Do We Feel and Touch?

How Do We Think?

How Do We Move?

Published by Raintree Steck-Vaughn Publishers,
an imprint of Steck-Vaughn Company

Library of Congress Cataloging-in-Publication Data
Ballard, Carol.
How do we think? / Carol Ballard.
p.   cm.—(How your body works)
Includes bibliographical references and index.
Summary: Describes the various parts of the brain and the nervous system and how they function to enable us to think, feel, move, and remember.
ISBN 0-8172-4740-8
1. Brain—Juvenile literature.
2. Nervous system—Juvenile literature.
3. Thought and thinking—Juvenile literature.
[1. Brain. 2. Nervous system.]
I. Title. II. Series.
QP376.B274   1998
612.8'2—dc21   97-17984

Printed in Italy. Bound in the United States.
1 2 3 4 5 6 7 8 9 0 02 01 00 99 98

Picture acknowledgments
The author and publishers thank the following for the use of their photographs:
All Action 11; Bubbles/James Lamb 23; Chris Fairclough Colour Library 6, 26; Zul Mukhida 16, 24, 25; M Murray/Format 27; Science Photo Library 12, 15, 20, 22, 28, 29 and Tony Stone 5. **Illustrators:** Kevin Jones Associates and Michael Courtney

Contents

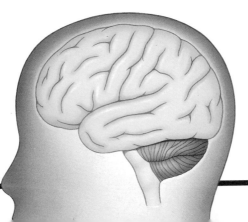

Thinking

If someone asked "How do we think?" you would probably say "We use our brains." This would be partly right, but the brain does not work alone.

▲
We are capable of many different thoughts.

In a computer system, the part that processes the information is no good by itself. It needs the rest of the system as well. It needs the keyboard, mouse, screen, and printer.

◄ The brain makes sure that all the parts of the body keep working smoothly.

4

In the same way, the brain needs the rest of the body—eyes, ears, fingertips, and muscles. The whole system is linked by a network of **nerves**, like the wires of a computer system.

This complicated system allows us to think and remember. It allows us to feel **emotions** and to sense the world around us. It controls the movements we make and the functions of our bodies.

People have many ▶ different emotions. We may feel happy or sad, frightened or relaxed, pleased or sorry.

What Does the Brain Do?

The brain allows us to do all the things we want to, such as walking, playing the piano, and riding a bicycle. These actions are called "**conscious**" actions. We know we are doing them and can decide when to start and stop.

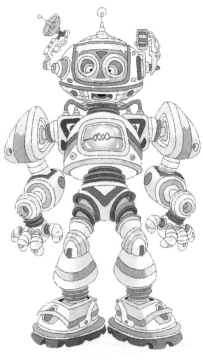

▲
Robots can do many things the human brain can do, but they do not have emotions or feelings.

The brain also controls "**subconscious**" actions. These actions keep our bodies working automatically, without thinking about them.

◀ While we are asleep, the brain makes sure that our hearts beat and that we breathe continuously.

We cannot control these actions or decide to start and stop them.

The brain creates feelings such as love, fear, and anger and collects and reads the information from our eyes, ears, skin, and muscles. Memories are stored in the brain, ready to be called up when we need them.

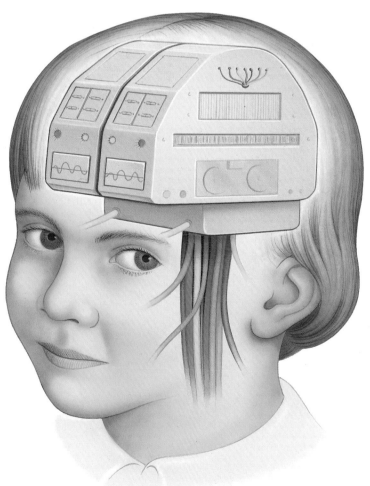

The brain is like the ▶ body's own computer. It controls everything we do.

What Is the Brain Made Of ?

The human brain weighs about 3.1 lbs. (1.4 kg) and is about the size of a small cauliflower. The brain is pinkish white and its surface is wrinkled. The skull bones provide a strong, protective case for the delicate brain. To keep the brain from hitting against the skull, it is surrounded by a layer of liquid.

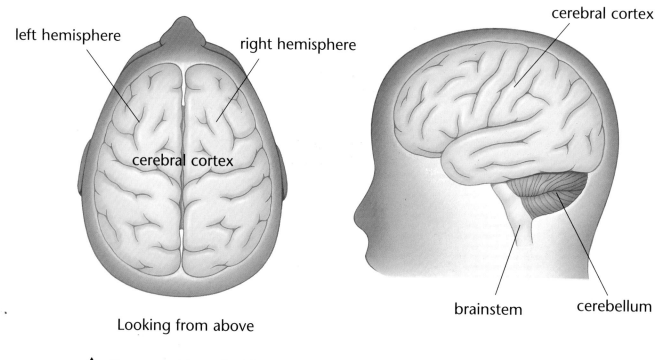

left hemisphere

right hemisphere

cerebral cortex

cerebral cortex

Looking from above

brainstem

cerebellum

▲ If you could see inside your head, your brain would look like this.

The brain is made up of millions of nerve cells called neurones. These are connected by tiny branches. Signals jump from nerve cell to nerve cell across these branches.

The brain has three parts. The cortex controls conscious actions and thinking. The **cerebellum** controls balance and coordination, and the brainstem controls heartbeat, breathing, and blood pressure.

first brain

second brain

▲ Some dinosaurs, like the Stegosaurus, had two brains—one in the head and the other at the start of the tail.

A Brain Map

Each area of the **cerebral** cortex, or brain center, is involved with its own specific actions or feelings. A brain map shows some of these areas. For example, the very front of the cerebral cortex controls thoughts and thinking. The area that controls sight and vision is at the back of the brain.

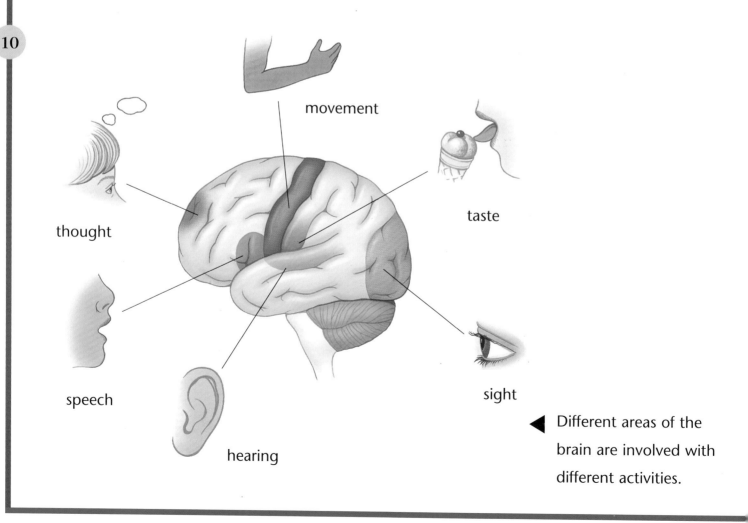

movement

thought

taste

speech

hearing

sight

◀ Different areas of the brain are involved with different activities.

Each hemisphere (half) of the brain controls one side of the body. The left hemisphere controls the right side of the body, and the right hemisphere controls the left side of the body.

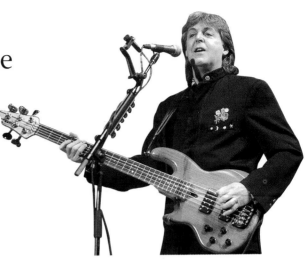

▲ Paul McCartney plays guitar with his left hand. Many famous artists and musicians are left-handed.

The two hemispheres of the cerebral cortex seem to be good at different tasks.

▲ The left side of the brain is good at working with words and numbers, while the right side is good at creative tasks such as music and art.

Brain and Nerves

Your brain is part of a network of nerves called the nervous system. You can think of the nervous system as having three parts, all linked together.

The first part is the brain and spinal cord, which make up the central nervous system (CNS). Messages travel to and from the body all the time along the CNS. The spinal cord is a bundle of nerve cells. To protect the spinal cord from damage it lies inside a channel made by the bones of the spine.

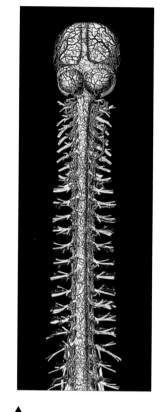

▲ Nerves connect every part of the body to the brain via the spinal cord.

◀ The spinal cord is protected by the bones of the spine.

The second part is the **sense organs** and nerve cells, which make up the peripheral nervous system (PNS). This collects information from your body and the world around you and sends messages to the CNS.

The third part of the nervous system is the automatic nervous system. All parts of your body are connected to the PNS, but some parts of your body function although you are not aware of them. These parts of the PNS are called the automatic nervous system (ANS).

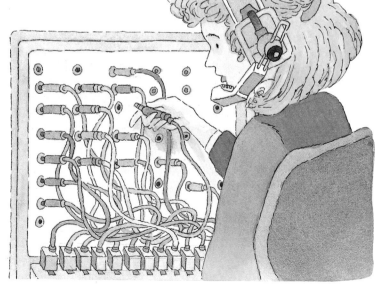

The brain receives and ▶ sends messages, like a busy telephone switchboard.

Information In and Out

Your nervous system is like a computer system. Information is put into a computer, using a mouse or keyboard, and the computer handles the information and sends results out to a screen. Information enters your nervous system through sense organs (such as eyes and ears) and from special cells that detect feelings such as heat and pain. The brain handles the information and the results are sent out to your muscles.

◀ We use our senses of hearing, sight, smell, taste, and touch to find out about the world around us.

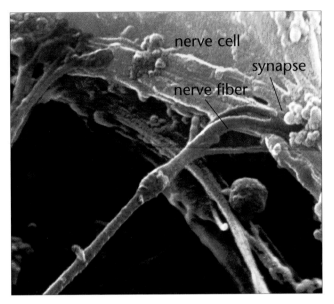

nerve cell

synapse

nerve fiber

▲

The junctions between nerve fibers and nerve cells are called synapses. They act like bridges.

In a computer system, all the information travels along wires. In the body, all the information travels along the nerve cells.

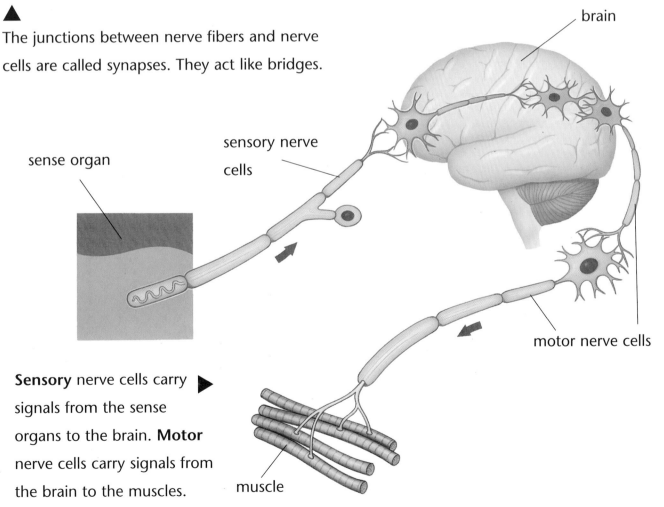

brain

sense organ

sensory nerve cells

motor nerve cells

Sensory nerve cells carry ▶ signals from the sense organs to the brain. **Motor** nerve cells carry signals from the brain to the muscles.

muscle

How Quick Are You?

We can all react very quickly when we need to. Try this activity with a friend to find out just how quickly you can react. You will need a 12-in. (30-cm) ruler for this activity.

Ask your friend to hold the ruler at the 12-in. (30 cm) end. Stand with your finger and thumb level with the 0—but do **not** touch the ruler.

When your friend lets go of the ruler, you must try to catch hold of it as quickly as you can.

◄ These children are testing their reaction times.

Look at the number between your finger and thumb where you caught the ruler. How many inches (cm) did the ruler drop before you caught it?

Try the test several times. Are your results always the same? Does it make any difference if you use your other hand?

Quick reactions can sometimes ▶ be very important!

Name	Right hand			Left hand		
	Test 1	2	3	Test 1	2	3
Me	4.5 in. (12 cm)	5.5 in. (14 cm)	6 in. (15 cm)	6.5 in. (16 cm)	6 in. (15 cm)	6.5 in. (16 cm)
Jane	4.5 in. (12 cm)	4 in. (10 cm)	4 in. (10 cm)	5.5 in. (14 cm)	6 in. (15 cm)	5.5 in. (14 cm)

▲ Record your results on a table like this.

Emergency Messages

Sometimes you need to react very quickly to avoid hurting yourself. Your body has a system especially designed to work faster than your normal reactions. In some **emergency** situations, the normal signal pathway is shortened and the brain is by-passed.

The signal travels from the sense organ to the spinal cord as usual, but it triggers a **reflex** reaction.

spinal cord

motor nerve pathway

muscle

sensory nerve ending in finger

In a reflex reaction, the signal by-passes the brain.

A signal travels straight from the spinal cord to the muscles to move your body out of danger. Your brain gets to know about the signals later, both the "in" signal from the sense organ and the "out" signal to the muscles.

▲
When the girl picks up the dish, receptors in her skin will send a signal to her brain telling it that the dish is hot!

19

Reflex reactions keep us from hurting ourselves. We cough automatically if something gets stuck in the windpipe, and blink if dirt gets into the eye.

A simple reflex action is the ▶ kneejerk. Tapping just below the kneecap makes the lower leg automatically jerk upward.

Awake and Asleep

Our brain keeps working while we sleep. Doctors use a medical machine called an encephalograph to follow patterns of brain signals. The patterns, or waves, are different when we are awake from when we are asleep.

▲

The **electrodes** on this girl's head provide doctors with information about her brain signals.

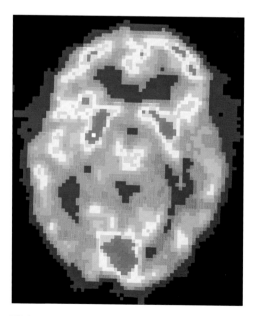

This **scan** shows the brain when we are awake. The areas that are busy are red.

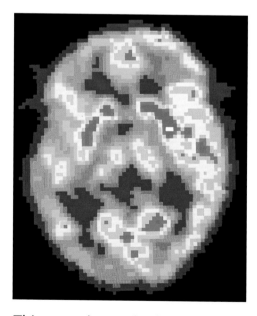

This scan shows the brain when we are sleeping. The areas that are not busy are blue.

Some people think that dreams help calm fears and worries about events that happened during the day. Other people think that dreams are the brain trying to make sense out of signals that occur while we sleep. People dream less as they get older. Babies probably spend about half of their sleeping time dreaming, but adults dream for less than one fifth of their sleeping time.

Our dreams are often made ▶ up of ordinary things jumbled together in unusual ways.

Memory

There are two kinds of memory, short-term and long-term. Short-term memories are memories we need to remember only for a short while, such as a message for somebody or a shopping list.

22

▲
Most people can remember something that happened when they were three or four years old.

Long-term memories are memories we want to remember forever. For example, once you have learned the colors of the rainbow, you will probably never forget them.

◀ **Roy G. Biv**. The letters in this silly name are the same as the first letters of the colors of the rainbow—Red, Orange, Yellow, Green, Blue, Indigo, Violet.

Doctors think that short-term memories stay in the cortex of the brain. To change them into long-term memories, signals travel from the cortex to the memory center deep inside the brain. They are stored here until they are needed.

Some elderly people can clearly remember things that happened long ago, but find it harder to remember recent events. ▼

Test Your Memory

Try this activity with a friend to find out just how good your memory is. You will need a collection of about twenty different objects on a tray.

These children are finding out how many objects they can remember.

▼

Ask your friend to choose twelve of the objects and to set them on the tray so that they can all be seen. (You must not watch!) When your friend is ready, look at the objects and try to concentrate as hard as you can. After one minute, look away and try to write down a list of all the objects on the tray.

Swap places and set the tray up for your friend. Did you both remember all the objects? Try it again with more objects on the tray this time.

25

▼ Playing the card game called Concentration tests your memory.

How Do We Learn?

To learn something, you first have to put it into your short-term memory. When your brain recognizes it as something you need forever, it is changed into a long-term memory. This is stored in the memory center deep in your brain until you want to remember it.

La sh monday
we went out
and was
some frienbs
and they mad
us lrfe

▲

Some people suffer from dyslexia, which means that they find reading and writing difficult. Words and letters appear jumbled, and sometimes they even seem to move about on the page.

◀ Schoolchildren today are often allowed a more active approach to lessons.

There are different ways of learning. Sometimes it helps to repeat a spelling or the steps needed to work out something again and again. Other things are easier to remember if you have worked them out for yourself. It often helps if you can link a new fact to something you already know.

▲ In Victorian schoolrooms, children learned their lessons by heart and then recited them to the teacher.

When Things Go Wrong

Headaches often have nothing to do with the brain. If muscles in the neck contract too much, blood cannot flow properly in the head. This makes the head ache.

▲
Banging your head can be painful! A hard knock may cause dizziness and a headache.

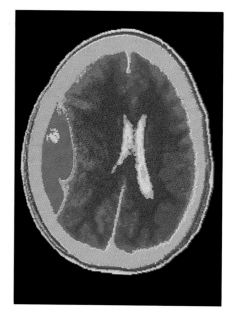

Banging the head may damage the brain. Often this damage is mild and temporary, but after a serious accident severe brain damage can occur.

◀ The red area on this brain scan shows a blood vessel that has burst. The bleeding is causing the brain to be squashed over to the right.

If the spinal cord is damaged in an accident, signals cannot travel between the brain and the rest of the body. People who have broken their necks are often unable to move their arms or legs.

Unlike other cells in the body, brain cells cannot be replaced when they die. When you are young this does not matter, because there are plenty of other, extra, cells to take their place. When people get older there are not as many extra cells, and this can cause problems such as forgetfulness.

Some children are born with an illness called cerebral palsy. They can think as well as anybody else, but because they find it difficult to control their movements, they need help with everyday activities. ▶

Glossary

cerebellum Area at the back of the brain that helps make movements smooth and coordinated.

cerebral To do with the brain.

conscious To be aware of something happening.

electrodes Wires through which electrical signals from the brain are given off.

emergency A dangerous situation that requires quick action.

emotions Strong feelings such as love and fear.

motor To do with movement.

nerves Stringlike parts inside the body that carry signals.

reflex When signals are sent to a body part without involving the brain.

scan Detailed picture of part of the body obtained by using a scanning machine.

sense organs Parts of the body that collect information, such as the eyes, ears, and nose.

sensory To do with feeling.

subconscious Actions in the body that we are not aware of.

Books to Read

Bailey, Donna. *All About Your Brain* (Health Facts). Austin, TX: Raintree Steck-Vaughn, 1990.

Bryan, Jenny. *Mind and Matter* (Bodyguards). Parsippany, NJ: Silver Burdett Press, 1993.

Funston, Sylvia. *It's All in Your Brain*. New York: Putnam Publishing Group, 1995.

Sandeman, Anna. *Your Body: Brain*. Danbury, CT: Franklin Watts, 1996.

Index